NATURE WATCH

BIRDS of PREY

Robin Kerrod

Consultant: Jemima Parry-Jones, MBE

LORENZ BOOKS

C O N

First published in 2000 by Lorenz Books
© Anness Publishing Limited 2000

Lorenz Books is an imprint of Anness Publishing Limited, Hermes House, 88–89 Blackfriars Road, London SE1 8HA.

Published in the USA by Lorenz Books, Anness Publishing Inc., 27 West 20th Street, New York, NY 10011; (800) 354–9657.

Distributed in Canada by Raincoast Books, 8680 Cambie Street, Vancouver, British Columbia, V6P 6M9.

ISBN 1 85967 641 3

A CIP catalogue record for this book is available from the British Library

Publisher: Joanna Lorenz
Managing Editor, Children's Books: Gilly Cameron Cooper
Senior Editor: Nicole Pearson
Editors: Linda Sonntag, Leon Gray
Designer: Ann Samuel
Picture Researcher: Gwen Campbell
Illustrators: Julian Baker, Vanessa Card, David Webb
Special Photography: Kim Taylor
Editorial Reader: Penelope Goodare
Production Controller: Yolande Denny
Printed and bound in Singapore

10 9 8 7 6 5 4 3 2 1

The birds of prey featured in this book are often described using their common English names first, followed by their Latin names in *italic*.

PICTURE CREDITS

b=bottom, t=top, c=centre, l=left, r=right

Heather Angel: 9bl, 21bl, 50br, 53bl, 59tl. Ardea: Ake Linday: 48bl / M. Watson: 32bl. BBC Natural History Unit: Bernard Castelein: 16tl, 55b / Nick Garbutt: 12tr / Tony Heald: 19tr, 34bl / David Kjaar: 49bl / Neil P. Lucas: 60br / Klaus Nigge: 22tr, 29tr, 62tl / Dietmar Nill: 7tr, 28bl / Pete Oxford: 28m / Chris Packham: 25m / Rico & Ruiz: 36bl, 41tl, 61m / Artur Tabor: 46bl / Richard du Toit: 11m, 12br / Tom Vezo: 25tl / Tom Walmsley: 25m. Bruce Coleman: Jane Burton: 42tl / Erik Bjurstrom: 56bl / John Cancalosi: 54tl / Robert P. Carr: 17tr / Jose Luis Gonzalez Grande: 11b, 3br, 46tl / Peter A. Hinchliffe: 9br / Steve Kaufman: 16br / Antonio Manzanares: 20tr, 37tr / Luiz Claudio Marigo: 33mr / George McCarthy: 30tl, 41m / Dr. Scott Nielsen: 55tr / Alan G. Potts: 5br, 43tl / Jeff Foot Productions: 17bl, 28tl / Hans Reinhard: 37m / John Shaw: 31br, 44bl / Kim Taylor: 43m / Rod Williams: 50tl / Gunter Ziesler: 2tr, 7tl. Ancient Art & Architecture Collection: 24bl. Planet Earth: Frank Blackburn: 36tr / John R. Bracegirdle: 25tl / Darroch Donald: 4bl / Carol Farneti- Foster: 51m / Nick Garbutt: 38tl, 58m, 58tr, 59tl, 59m, 59bl / Ken Lucas: 47tl / Andrew Mounter: 56br / Susan & Alan Parker: 2br, 6br / Johan le Roux: 45ml / Keith Scholey: 52tr / Jonathan Scott: 53tl, 35br / Anup & Manoj Shah: 54m. Ecoscene: Ian Beames: 59m / Robert Walker: 58m. Mary Evans: 5b, 15tl, 17br, 21tr, 50bl, 59bl. Oxford Scientific Films: Miriam Austerman: 64bl, 35br, 60tr / Adrian Bailey: 52br / Bob Bennett: 10bl / G I Bernard: 19br, 54br / Mike Birkhead: 60bl / Tony & Liz Bomford: 41bl / David Cayless: 61bl / Susan Day: 61tl / John Downer: 55m / Carol Farneti-Foster: 13tr / David B. Fleetham: 47br / Dennis Green: 37br / Mark Hamblin:19tl, 64tl, 45mr / Mike Hill: 49tr / Tim Jackson: 25tr, endpaper / Lon E. Lauber: 7m, 52tl / Michael Leach:5tr, 6tr, 47ml, 24tr / Ted Levin: 29bl, 49tr / Rob Nunnington: 12bl / Ben Osborne: 55m / Stan Osolinski: 6bl, 2tl,7br,18b, 35tr, 34tl, 63br, 52bl / Mike Price: 51tl / Norbert Rosing: 47tr / Frank Scheidermeyer: 35bl / David Tipling:: 58tl / David Thompson: 25tr / Barbara Tyack: 55tl / Konrad Wothe: 5tr, 20bl. FLPA: J J Hinojosa: 44tr. Michael Holford: 3tla. Gallo Images: Anthony Bannister: 8tr, 11tl, 29tl / Nigel Dennis: 29br, 52br, 62bl. 37bl, 45br, 51bl / Clem Haagner: 21m, 25bl, 40tr, 45tr, 51tr / Hein von Horsten: 55tl, 40tl / M. Philip Kahl: 53ml / Peter Lillie: 43tl / Eric Reisinger: 21tl. Images Colour Library: cover, 14-15, 26-27, 50-31, 58-59, 52-53. NHPA: Stephen Dalton: 13m, 63tl / Manfred Danegger: 22b / Martin Harvey: 49br / William Paton: 23b. Papilio: 10tr, 24m. David Pike: 50b, 31bl, 51tl, 31tr. Kim Taylor: 5tl, 9tr, 14br, 14bl, 14tl, 15bl, 15tr, 17tl, 62br, 18tl, 27m, 27tl, 1 full page, 26tl, 26tr, 27br. Warren Photographic: Jane Burton: 42ml, 42m, 42mr / Kim Taylor: 4-5m, 15br 19bl, 57tl, 57tr.

Thanks to the National Birds of Prey Centre in Newent for their help in creating this book.

WHAT IS A BIRD OF PREY?

HUNTING

TENTS

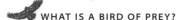
What is a Bird of Prey?

There are nearly 9,000 different species of birds in the world. Most of them eat plant shoots, seeds, nuts and fruit, or small creatures such as insects and worms. However, around 400 species, called birds of prey, hunt prey with their feet or scavenge carrion (the flesh of dead animals). Birds of prey are called raptors, from the Latin *rapere* meaning "to scize", because they grip and kill their prey with sharp talons and hooked beaks. The majority of raptors hunt by day. They are called diurnal birds of prey. Day hunters include eagles, falcons and hawks, and vultures (which are scavengers). Other raptors, such as owls, are nocturnal, which means they are active at night.

▼ HANGING AROUND

The outstretched wings of the kestrel (*Falco tinnunculus*) face into the wind as the bird hovers above a patch of ground in search of prey. The bird also spreads its broad tail to supplement the air-catching effect of its wings.

Large, forward-facing eyes

Hooked, powerful, bill

▼ IN A LEAGUE OF THEIR OWN

Five young tawny owls cluster together on a branch. Owls are not closely related to the other birds of prey. They usually hunt by night instead of during the day. However, they do share certain features with the other birds of prey. They have excellent eyesight for spotting prey, sharp, hooked beaks (bills) for ripping flesh, and strong legs, with pointed, curled claws (talons) for gripping their prey.

Tawny owls
(*Strix aluco*)

◄ HAWKEYE
The sparrowhawk has large eyes that face forwards. The bill is hooked, for tearing flesh. These are typical features of daytime hunters.

Eurasian sparrowhawk
(*Accipiter nisus*)

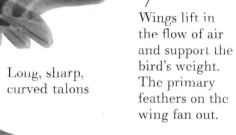

Wings lift in the flow of air and support the bird's weight. The primary feathers on the wing fan out.

Long, sharp, curved talons

Tail guides the bird through the air and also acts as a brake

▲ BUILT FOR SPEED
The peregrine falcon is the one of the swiftest birds in the world, able to dive at up to 224 km/h. Its swept-back wings help it cut through the air at speed. Their shape has been copied by aircraft designers for the wings of fighter planes.

▼ THE EAGLE HAS LANDED
In the snow-covered highlands of Scotland, a golden eagle stands over a rabbit it has just killed. Eagles kill with their talons. They are so long, sharp and deeply curved that one swipe is usually enough to kill the rabbit.

Golden eagle
(*Aquila chrysaetos*)

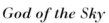

God of the Sky
Horus was one of the most important gods in ancient Egypt. He was the god of the sky and the heavens. His sacred bird was the falcon, and Horus is often represented with a human body and a falcon's head. The Egyptian hieroglyph (picture symbol) for "god" in ancient Egyptian is a falcon.

Shapes and Sizes

There are huge differences in size among birds of prey. As many as 40 pygmy falcons could perch on the outstretched wings of one Andean condor. Pygmy falcons are the smallest birds of prey, measuring as little as 20 centimetres from head to tail. The Andean condor is the biggest bird of prey, with a wingspan of some 3 metres. In most species, the female is larger than the male. In fact, in some hawk and falcon species the females are up to 50 per cent bigger than the males. This is called reverse sexual dimorphism. Most raptors look quite similar when they perch. When they fly, however, there is a great variation in wing size and shape. This usually reflects the different techniques they adopt when hunting prey and the nature of their habitat. For example, the huge wings of the Andean condor allow it to soar high above the Andes mountains.

Little owl
(*Athene noctua*)

▲ **WELL-ROUNDED**
The little owl, like other owls, has a round head and broad, rounded wings. Its body, too, has a well-rounded shape, because of its fairly loose covering of feathers. It appears to have no neck at all. The little owl is about 23 cm from head to tail.

▲ **AMERICAN SCAVENGER**
The turkey vulture (or turkey buzzard) is a small vulture that lives in North and South America. It grows up to 80 cm from head to tail.

▶ **DIFFERENT SIZES**
The female sparrowhawk can grow up to about 38 cm from head to tail. The male bird (shown here) is much smaller, reaching only about 28 cm from head to tail.

Eurasian sparrowhawk
(*Accipiter nisus*)

► THE BIGGEST

The magnificent Andean condor is the biggest of all birds of prey. The males grow up to 1.3 m from head to tail and can weigh more than 12 kg. The condor is a scavenger, which means that it feeds on dead animals rather than hunting live prey.

Andean condor (*Vultur gryphus*)

Did you know? A pygmy owl's body is as long as an eagle's ear tufts.

▲ COMMON BUTEOS

This common buzzard (*Buteo buteo*) is typical of the family of birds of prey known as buteos. Buteos are about 50 cm from head to tail and have long, broad wings up to 1.3 m from wing tip to wing tip. This bird is commonly found gliding high above the grasslands and woodlands of Europe and Asia in search of small mammals and reptiles.

▲ FISH-EATING EAGLE

The bald eagle (*Haliaeetus leucocephalus*) is instantly recognizable by its snowy white head and tail. It is an impressive bird, growing up to 1 m from head to tail. The bird's long talons enable it to pluck fish from the surface of rivers and lakes in North America.

► STANDING TALL

The tallest and most unusual bird of prey is the secretary bird of Africa. It stands up to 1.2 m tall, and its wings can span more than 2 m. It can soar in the sky like other birds of prey, but most of the time it walks on the ground on its long legs.

Secretary bird (*Sagittarius serpentarius*)

How the Body Works

Birds of prey are supreme fliers. Like other birds, they have powerful chest and wing muscles to move their wings. Virtually the whole body is covered with feathers to make it smooth and streamlined and able to slip easily through the air. The bones are very light, and some have a honeycomb structure, which makes them lighter still. Birds of prey differ from other birds in a number of ways, particularly in their powerful bills (beaks) and feet, which are well adapted for their life as hunters. Also unlike most other birds, they regurgitate (cough up) pellets. These contain the parts of their prey they cannot digest.

▲ **NAKED NECK**
A Ruppell's vulture feeds on a zebra carcass in the Masai Mara region of eastern Africa. Like many vultures, it has a naked neck, which it can thrust deep inside the carcass. As a result, it can feed without getting its feathers too covered in blood.

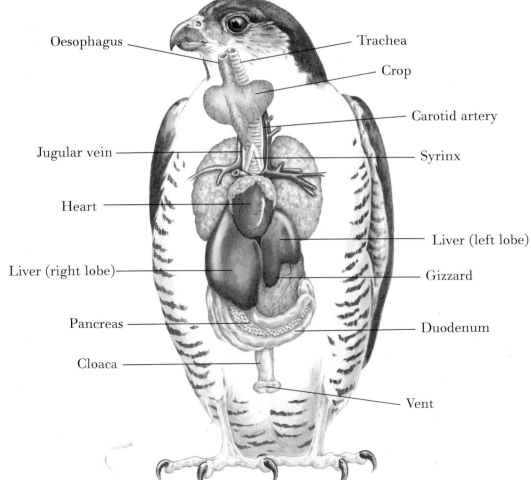

Oesophagus
Trachea
Crop
Carotid artery
Jugular vein
Syrinx
Heart
Liver (left lobe)
Liver (right lobe)
Gizzard
Pancreas
Duodenum
Cloaca
Vent

◄ **BODY PARTS**
Underneath their feathery covering, birds of prey have a complex system of internal organs. Unlike humans, most birds have a crop to store food in before digestion. They also have a gizzard to grind up hard particles of food, such as bone, and to start the process of making a pellet. Birds also have a syrinx (the bird equivalent of the human vocal cord).

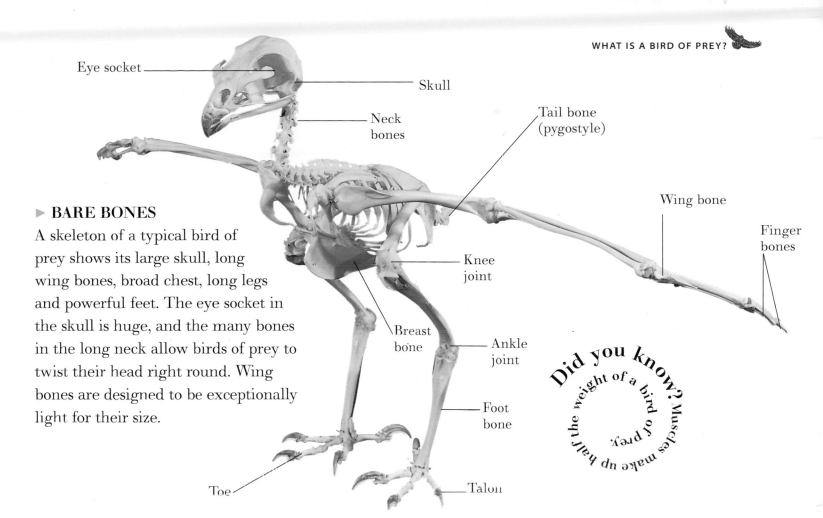

Eye socket

Skull

Neck bones

Tail bone (pygostyle)

Wing bone

Finger bones

Knee joint

Breast bone

Ankle joint

Foot bone

Toe

Talon

▶ BARE BONES

A skeleton of a typical bird of prey shows its large skull, long wing bones, broad chest, long legs and powerful feet. The eye socket in the skull is huge, and the many bones in the long neck allow birds of prey to twist their head right round. Wing bones are designed to be exceptionally light for their size.

Did you know? Muscles make up half the weight of a bird of prey.

▼ BACK TO FRONT

This peregrine falcon appears to have eyes in the back of its head! Its body is facing away, but its eyes are looking straight into the camera. All birds of prey can twist their heads right round like this, because they have many more vertebrae than mammals. They can see in any direction without moving the body, but they cannot move their eyeballs in their sockets.

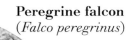

Peregrine falcon
(*Falco peregrinus*)

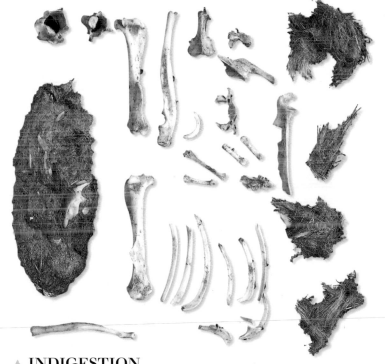

▲ INDIGESTION

On the left of the picture above is the regurgitated (coughed-up) pellet of a barn owl, and on the right are the indigestible parts it contained. The pellet is about 5 cm long. From its contents we can tell that the owl has just eaten a small mammal, because the pellet contains scraps of fur and fragments of bone.

The Senses

Humans rely on five senses to find out about the world. They are sight, hearing, smell, taste and touch. However, most birds live using just the two senses of sight and hearing. In birds of prey, sight is by far the most important sense for finding and hunting the prey they need to survive. Their eyes are exceptionally large in relation to the size of their head, and they are set in the skull so that they look forwards. This binocular (two-eyed) forward vision enables them to judge distances accurately when hunting. Owls have particularly large eyes that are well adapted for seeing in dim light. They are equally dependent on hearing to find prey in the dark. Some harriers and hawks use their keen sense of hearing to hunt, too. Birds' ear openings are quite small. They are set back from the eyes and cannot be seen because they are covered in feathers.

Common buzzard (*Buteo buteo*)

▲ **OPEN WIDE**
A common buzzard opens its mouth wide to make its distinctive mewing call. This bird has extremely large eyes in relation to its body, so it has excellent eyesight. The forward-facing eyes give it good stereoscopic (3D) vision and the ability to pinpoint the exact position of a mouse in the grass 100 m away.

◄ **NOT TO BE SNIFFED AT**
The turkey vulture of North and South America, like all New World vultures, has nostrils that you can see right through. Its nose is very sensitive. This enables the turkey vulture to sniff carrion on the ground while it is flying above the forest canopy.

Turkey vulture (*Cathartes aura*)

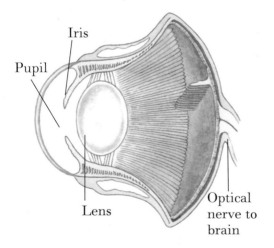

Iris

Pupil

Lens

Optical nerve to brain

▲ **OWL EYE**
The owl has exceptional eyesight. Its eye is very long, unlike the spherical human eye. The tubular shape of the owl's eye allows it to spot its prey from far away.

Spotted eagle owl (*Bubo africanus*)

◄ **FORWARD FACE**

The African spotted eagle owl has big eyes. The pupil (centre) and lens are especially large to allow more light to enter and provide the owl with good night vision. The eyes are set in a flat facial disc. The earlike projections on top of the owl's head are actually ornamental tufts of feathers used for display. The true ears are hidden under stiff feathers at either side of the facial disc. They are sensitive to the slightest noise, which helps the owl locate its prey in the dark.

► **ON THE LOOKOUT**

This large falcon, called a lanner, is soaring high in the sky on outstretched wings, looking down with its sharp eyes on the scene below. If the lanner sees a flying bird, it will fold back its wings and dive on the unsuspecting bird. The lanner will hit the bird at high speed and usually break its neck. Then it will either snatch the bird in mid-air or pick it up off the ground.

◄ **MONTAGU'S EYEBROW**

Montagu's harrier is a slender, long-legged hawk with an owl-like facial ruff. The eyes are surrounded by a small bony ridge covered in feathers, called a supraorbital ridge. It probably helps protect the harrier's eyes from attack when the bird goes hunting, and may also act as a shield against the sun's rays when it is flying.

Montagu's harrier
(*Circus pygargus*)

11

Wings and Flight

The wings of most birds work in the same way. Strong pectoral (chest) muscles make the wings flap and drive the bird through the air. As it moves, the wings lift in the flow of air and support the bird's weight. The bird is now flying. All birds have differently shaped wings that are adapted to their way of life. Large birds of prey, such as vultures, spend much of their time soaring high in the sky. These birds have long, broad wings that glide on air currents. The smaller hawks, such as the sparrowhawk, have short, rounded wings and a long tail for rapid, zigzagging flight through woodland habitats. A bird's tail is also important for flying. It acts much like a ship's rudder, steadying the bird's body and guiding it through the air. It can be fanned out to give extra lift and also helps the bird to slow down when landing.

▲ **WING FINGERS**
An African fish eagle takes to the air. Like other eagles, it has broad wings and fingered wing tips, seen plainly here. The "fingers" reduce air turbulence around the wings, giving better lift.

Mauritius kestrel
(*Falco punctatus*)

▲ **AGILE BIRD**
The Mauritius kestrel has a broad tail and, for a falcon, fairly short wings. These two features help it to manoeuvre well in the woodland habitat in which it lives. It lives on the island of Mauritius, in the Indian Ocean.

▲ **DROPPING IN**
A sparrowhawk (*Accipter nisus*) is poised to seize a bird it has just spotted. It has short, rounded wings and a long tail. The sparrowhawk's wings beat rapidly and provide enough speed to surprise its unsuspecting prey.

Eagle of the Gods

In Greek mythology, the eagle was the favoured bird of the mighty Zeus. Zeus was god of the sky, lord of the winds and rains, and king among the gods. He is often depicted holding a thunderbolt in his right hand, with an eagle standing at his feet. Here we see him riding in a chariot, drawn by a pair of his sacred birds.

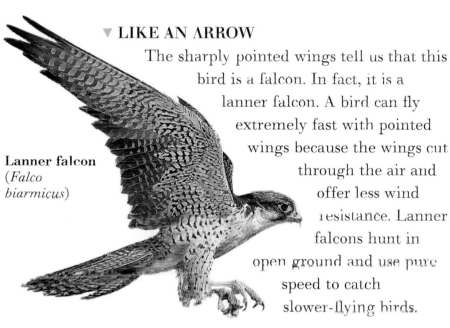

▼ LIKE AN ARROW

The sharply pointed wings tell us that this bird is a falcon. In fact, it is a lanner falcon. A bird can fly extremely fast with pointed wings because the wings cut through the air and offer less wind resistance. Lanner falcons hunt in open ground and use pure speed to catch slower-flying birds.

Lanner falcon
(*Falco biarmicus*)

▲ BUILT TO SOAR

A white-backed vulture soars high in the sky with its broad wings fully outstretched on the lookout for carcasses on the ground. In the right climate, the vulture can remain in the air for a long time, because its wings provide plenty of lift.

► READY, STEADY, GO

A young male kestrel takes off in a multiple-exposure photograph. First the bird thrusts its body forwards and raises its wings. Its wings extend and beat downwards, pushing slightly backwards. As the air is forced back, the bird is driven forwards. At the same time, air moving past the wings gives the bird the lift it needs to keep itself airborne.

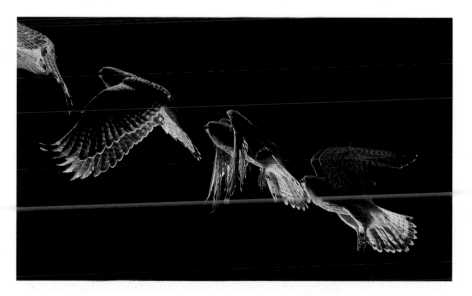

Focus on

1 A Harris' hawk (*Parabuteo unicinctus*) perches on a branch on the lookout for prey such as reptiles and small mammals. This native of South and Central America and the southern United States is also called the bay-winged hawk because of the rust-brown (bay) bars on its shoulders. It has the relatively short, rounded wings and long tail typical of most small hawks.

Most of the smaller species of hawk have developed wings that enable them to fly at fast speeds over short distances. Larger hawks have broader, longer wings. These allow the birds to soar and glide in the air whilst scanning the ground below for their prey. Every species favours a different flying technique. For example, sparrowhawks twist and turn with ease as they manoeuvre among the many trees in the woodlands in which they are found. High-speed photography allows us to follow the action as the Harris' hawk shown here takes to the air.

2 Now the hawk is getting ready to fly. It leans forwards and begins to raise its wings. It tenses its leg muscles, ready to thrust itself from the perch. The bird's distinctive red thighs and white rump, and the white patches on the underwing, are clearly visible.

3 The hawk lifts its wings, and the primaries (the flight feathers at the end of the wings) fan out. It pushes its legs against the perch to take off.

Hawk Flight

4 With a powerful downbeat of its wings and a final push with its legs, the hawk thrusts its body from the perch and begins to travel forwards through the air. As the air flows past the wings, it makes them lift and so supports the bird's body. The tail fans out and downwards to provide extra lift. The bird is now airborne.

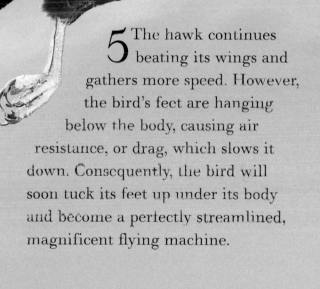

5 The hawk continues beating its wings and gathers more speed. However, the bird's feet are hanging below the body, causing air resistance, or drag, which slows it down. Consequently, the bird will soon tuck its feet up under its body and become a perfectly streamlined, magnificent flying machine.

Did you know? Sacs in a bird's body fill with air to help it stay airborne.

Bill and Talons

The bill and talons of birds of prey are well adapted for killing and feeding on prey or scavenging on the remains of carcasses. Typically the bill is hooked and sharp. However, it is not generally used for killing, but for tearing flesh. Raptors also use their bills to pluck the feathers from birds they catch. Most birds of prey use their feet for the kill. Their toes are tipped with long, sharp, curved talons. When a bird swoops on its prey, the toes clamp round the prey's body and the talons sink into the flesh. The prey is quickly crushed to death. Small birds of prey, such as many falcon species, have less powerful leg muscles and may not always kill their prey this way. So the bird may have to finish it off with a bite. For this purpose, they have a notch (called a tomial tooth) in the upper part of the bill.

Indian honey buzzard (*Pernis ptilorhyncus*)

▲ INSECT-EATER

The bill of the Indian honey buzzard is relatively small and delicate compared with that of most other birds of prey. The honey buzzard has no need for a strong bill because it feeds mainly on insects and the larvae of wasps and bees.

▶ EGG HEAD

The Egyptian vulture's hooked bill is too weak to break into a large carcass without the aid of larger vultures. However, its long bill is ideal for breaking eggs, one of its favourite foods. In contrast to this bird's fine head plummage, other vultures have bare heads and necks. This prevents them from covering their feathers with blood when they reach deep inside a carcass to feed.

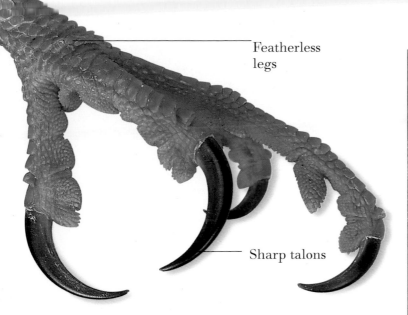

Featherless legs

Sharp talons

▲ SPINDLY LEGS

The legs of the sparrowhawk are long and slender and lack feathers. Both the toes and talons are long. As it homes in on a small bird, the sparrowhawk thrusts its legs forwards, with both feet spread wide. It then snaps its toes and talons around the prey's body, and captures it in a deadly grip. The sparrowhawk then flies off to land and feed on its catch.

▲ FEATHER TROUSERS

Like most owls, the great horned owl of North America has soft feathers covering its legs and feet, as well as its body. They help keep its flight silent.

▲ FEET FIRST

The strong feet of the American bald eagle are geared to catching fish, the main part of the bird's diet. Its talons are sharp and curved. The American bald eagle's feet are powerful enough to cope with a struggling pacific salmon, sometimes weighing as much as the bird itself.

Horrific Harpies
The harpy eagle is one of the most formidable birds of prey. It takes its name from the Harpies of Greek mythology. These were winged monsters that brought violent winds. They had women's heads, pale with hunger, and the bodies and sharp talons of eagles. They attacked people and stole or fouled their food.

Hunting on the Wing

Sparrowhawk
(*Accipiter
nisus*)

Birds of prey hunt in different ways.
Many smaller raptors and owls sit on a
perch and simply wait for a meal to
appear on the ground or fly past. This is
called still hunting. Other birds search for
prey by flying low over the open ground, or
in and out of cover, such as a clump of
trees. Kestrels are among the birds that
hover in the air while looking for prey, and
then swoop down suddenly on it. On the
other hand, peregrines are noted for their
spectacular dives, or stoops. With wings almost
folded, they dive on their prey from a great
height, accelerating up to hundreds of kilometres
an hour. Their aim is to strike the prey at high
speed to kill it instantly. The
peregrine either snatches
its prey from the air, or
picks it up off the ground.

▲ SURPRISE, SURPRISE
The sparrowhawk uses
surprise and speed to make a
kill. It flies under cover until
it spots a potential meal,
then dashes out
into the open to
snatch up its
unsuspecting
prey at speed.

◄ PLUCKY EAGLE
An American bald eagle plucks a cattle egret
it has just killed, making a change from
its usual diet of fish. Most birds of prey
pluck the feathers from birds they
have caught before eating, as
they cannot digest them.
Owls are the only birds
to swallow their
prey whole.

Bald eagle
(*Haliaeetus
leucocephalus*)

18

Buzzard
(Buteo buteo)

◄ RABBIT RELISH

A common buzzard stands guard over the rabbit it has just killed. Over grassland, the buzzard hunts on the wing, sometimes hovering like a kestrel. Where there are trees or rocks, it may perch on a high point for hours until it sights prey. The buzzard then swoops down quickly upon it.

▲ IN HOT PURSUIT

An African harrier hawk chases doves along the riverbank. Such chases more often than not end in failure. This hawk is about the same size as a typical harrier, but it has longer wings.

▼ IT'S A COVER-UP

Spreading out its wings, a kestrel tries to cover up the mouse it is preparing to eat on its feeding post. This behaviour is known as mantling, and is common among birds of prey. They do it to hide their food from other hungry birds, in case they try to rob them.

▼ MAKING A MEAL OF IT

A kestrel tucks into its kill on its favourite feeding post. The bird holds the prey with its feet and claws and tears the flesh into small pieces with its sharp bill. It swallows small bones, but often discards big ones. Later it regurgitates (brings up) pellets containing the bits of its prey it was unable to digest.

Kestrel
(Falco tinnunculus)

The Hunted

Birds of prey hunt all kinds of animals. Many prey on other birds, including sparrows, starlings and pigeons, which are usually taken in the air. Certain birds prey on small mammals, such as rabbits, lemmings, rats, mice and voles, and some of the larger eagles will even take larger mammals. The Philippine eagle and the harpy eagles of South America pluck monkeys from the rainforest canopy. These eagles are massive birds, with bodies a metre long. Serpent eagles and secretary birds feast on snakes and other reptiles. Small birds of prey often feed on insects and worms. Most species will also supplement their diet by scavenging on carrion (the meat of dead animals) whenever they find it.

▲ INSECT INSIDE

A lesser kestrel prepares to eat a grasshopper it has just caught on a rooftop in Spain. This kestrel lives mainly on insects. It catches grasshoppers and beetles on the ground, and all kinds of flying insects whilst in flight. When there are plenty of insects, flocks of lesser kestrels feed together. Unlike the larger common kestrel, the lesser kestrel does not hover when hunting.

Golden eagle
(*Aquila chrysaetos*)

◄ GOLDEN HUNTER

A golden eagle stands guard over the squirrel it has just caught. The golden eagle usually hunts low down. It flushes out prey — mainly rabbits, hares and grouse, which it catches and kills on the ground. Whenever they get the chance, golden eagles will also eat carrion.

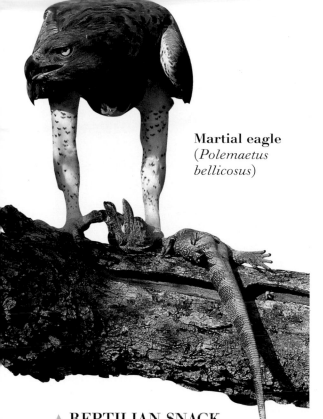

Martial eagle
(*Polemaetus bellicosus*)

▲ REPTILIAN SNACK

A martial eagle stands over its lizard kill in the Kruger National Park, South Africa. This is Africa's biggest eagle, capable of taking prey as big as a kuda (a small antelope).

▼ SNAIL SPECIALIST

A snail kite eyes its next meal. This is the most specialist feeder among birds of prey, eating only freshwater snails. It breeds in the Everglades National Park, Florida, USA.

Did you know? 12 species of birds of prey eat only insects.

The Fabulous Roc
In the famous tales of The Arabian Nights, Sinbad the Sailor encountered enormous birds called rocs. They looked like eagles, but were gigantic in size, and preyed on elephants and other large beasts. In this picture, the fearsome rocs are dropping huge boulders on Sinbad's ship in an attempt to finally destroy him.

▲ COBRA KILLER

A pale chanting goshawk has caught and killed a yellow cobra. The chanting goshawks earned their name because of their noisy calls in the breeding season. The African plains are the hunting grounds of both the pale and the dark chanting goshawks, which feed mainly on reptiles, such as lizards and snakes.

Snail kite
(*Rostrhamus sociabilis*)

Feuding and Fighting

Birds often squabble over food. Some birds of prey harry (intimidate) other raptors that have already made a kill and try to force them to drop it. This behaviour is called piracy. Sometimes birds of prey are attacked by the birds that they often prey on. A number of small birds may join forces against a larger adversary and give chase, usually calling loudly. This is known as mobbing and it generally serves to confuse and irritate the raptor and also warns off other prey in the area.

Birds of prey must also defend their nests against predators. The eggs and chicks of harriers and other ground-nesting raptors are especially vulnerable to attack. Nesting adults will often fly at intruders and try to chase them off.

▲ **SCRAP IN THE SNOW**
On the snowy shores of the Kamchatka Peninsula, in northeast Russia, these sea eagles are fighting over a fish. A Steller's sea eagle, the biggest of all sea eagles, is shown on the right, with its huge wings outstretched. Its opponents, struggling in the snow, are white-tailed eagles. The two kinds of sea eagles are bound to meet and fight, because they occupy a similar habitat and feed on similar prey – fish, birds and small mammals.

◀ **FISH FIGHT**
Two common buzzards fight over a fish they have both spotted. Buzzards do not go fishing like ospreys, but they will feed on dead fish washed up on river banks. Buzzards, like many other raptors, will eat carrion as well as their preferred food of small mammals, such as rabbits, and the worms and beetles they find on the ground.

Common buzzards
(*Buteo buteo*)

▶ UNDER THREAT

On the plains of Africa, a dead animal carcass attracts not only vultures, but other scavengers as well. Here, a jackal is trying to get a look-in, but a lappet-faced vulture is warning it off with outstretched wings.

Did you know? Hunters once used eagle owls as bait to attract mobbing birds into range.

Jay
(*Garrulus glandarius*)

▲ CLEVER MIMIC

When a jay spots a predator, such as a bird of prey, it gives out an alarm call or mimics the predator's own call to warn off other jays.

▲ IN HOT PURSUIT

An osprey has seen this pelican dive into the water and assumes that it now has a fish in its pouch. So it gives chase. Time and again, the osprey will fly straight at the pelican and scare it so much that it will finally release the fish from its pouch.

▼ SAFETY IN NUMBERS

A number of crows have ganged up to mob a steppe eagle. They are bold enough to perch dangerously close to their enemy, calling loudly to persuade it to move on. Although the eagle would be more than a match for its tormentors, it might fly off just to escape aggravation.

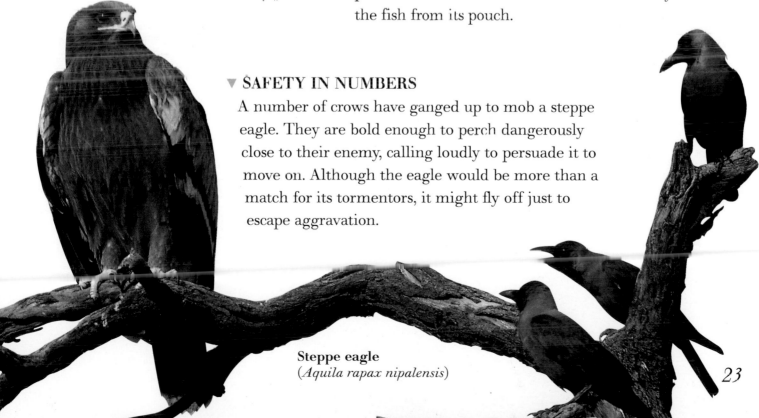

Steppe eagle
(*Aquila rapax nipalensis*)

23

The Night Hunters

Owls are the supreme night hunters, their bodies well adapted for hunting in the dark. For one thing, they fly silently. The flight feathers on their wings are covered with a fine down to muffle the sound of air passing through them. The owl's eyes are particularly adapted for night vision. They contain many more rods than the eyes of other species. Rods are the structures that make eyes sensitive to light. The owl's hearing is superb, too. The rings of fine feathers owls have around each eye help channel sounds into the ears. The ears themselves are surrounded by flaps of skin that can be moved to pinpoint exactly the sources of sounds. A few other raptors also hunt after sundown. They include the bat hawk of Africa and Asia, which eats bats, swallows and insects whilst in flight.

▲ GET A GRIP
Like all owls, the barn owl has powerful claws for attacking and gripping prey. The outer toe can be moved backwards and forwards to change grip.

Wise Owl
For centuries, owls have had a reputation for being wise birds. This came about because in Greek mythology, the little owl was the sacred bird of the goddess of wisdom, Athena. She gave her name to Greece's capital city, Athens. The best-known coin of the ancient Greek world was issued in Athens and featured an owl.

▲ ROUNDHEAD
Of all the owls, the barn owl has the most prominent round face – properly called a facial disc. This gives it a rather ghostly appearance. The disc is formed of short, stiff feathers.

▲ BIG OWL

A European eagle owl stands over a red fox left for it as bait. It looks round warily before beginning to eat. The eagle owl is a fierce predator, and will hunt prey as big as a young roe deer. It is a large bird, growing up to 70 cm long, powerfully built, and with long ear tufts.

▼ MOUTHFUL

A barn owl carries off a mouse it has just caught. Owls carry prey in their bills, unlike the other birds of prey, which carry it in their claws. Barn owls are found throughout most of the world and in many kinds of habitat – moorland, desert, forest and farmland.

Barn owl
(*Tyto alba*)

► WHAT A HOOTER

A mouse is carried off by a tawny owl. The long hooting call of the tawny owl can be heard in woodlands, parks and gardens across Europe.

▲ PEEKABOO

A burrowing owl peers out of its nest hole. These small, long-legged birds live in the prairies and grasslands of the New World, from Canada to the tip of South America. They often take over the abandoned holes of other burrowers, such as prairie dogs.

25

Focus on

1 This owl is waiting for a rustle in the undergrowth. Suddenly it hears something. It swivels its head, and its sensitive ears pinpoint exactly where the sound is coming from. Then it sees a mouse, rummaging among the leaf litter on the ground for grubs and insects.

2 Keeping its eyes glued on its potential meal, the owl launches itself into the air. It brings its body forwards, pushes off the post with its feet and opens its wings. Just a few metres away, the mouse carries on rummaging for food. It has heard nothing and is busy searching out a tasty insect in the leaf litter on the ground.

The barn owl is found on all continents except Antarctica. It is easily recognizable because of its white, heart-shaped facial disc. Its eyes are relatively small for an owl, but it can still see well at night. It hunts as much by ear as by eye. Its hearing is particularly keen, because the feathers on its exceptionally well-developed facial disc channel sounds into its ears with great precision. The owl featured here is "still-hunting", watching for prey from a favourite perch. However, barn owls often hunt while flying. They cruise slowly and silently back and forth over their feeding grounds until they hear or spy prey, then swoop down silently for the kill.

the Silent Swoop

3 The owl makes a beeline for its prey with powerful beats of its wings. Even though it is travelling quite fast, it still makes no sound. The owl has dense, soft feathers covering its wings and legs. These feathers silence the flow of air as it passes through them. This helps the owl to muffle its flight and to concentrate on the sounds that the mouse makes as the bird draws closer to its prey.

5 Now only a few centimetres above the ground, the owl thrusts its feet forwards, claws spread wide, and drops on to its prey. At the same time, it spreads out its wings and tail to slow down its approach. The hunter's aim is deadly. Its talons close round the mouse and crush it to death. Then the owl picks up the dead mouse in its beak and returns to its perch. The owl will swallow the mouse head-first.

4 The mouse at last begins to sense that something is wrong as the owl approaches. For an instant it is glued to the spot in fear. Then it starts to run for its life. However, the owl is more than a match for it. With its rounded wings and broad tail, it is able to twist and turn in the air with ease, following every change of direction of the scuttling mouse.

Fishing Birds

Many birds of prey will eat dead fish when they find it on the river bank and shore. However, some specialize in plucking live fish from the water. Outstanding among the fishing birds is the osprey, found around rivers and lakes throughout the world, except in the polar regions. In many areas, the osprey competes for its food with various species of sea or fish eagles, such as the magnificent bald eagle of North America. All these fishing raptors are large. They have strong, arched bills, long talons, and rough scales on their feet, which help them grip their slippery prey. Their pale underparts imitate the bright sky and camouflage them from the fish below.

▲ BALD FISHER
An American bald eagle rests on a branch with a fish it has killed. It is the only fishing eagle in the Americas. The white feathers on its head and neck make the bird look bald from a distance.

▲ FISH OWL
Some owls go fishing, too. This Pel's fishing owl, from Africa, is standing with its catch. Like other fishing owls, it has no ear tufts. Its talons are sharp and curved to catch slippery fish.

◄ WELL CAUGHT
An osprey kicks up spray as it grabs at a fish swimming just below the surface of the water. Sometimes ospreys take fish as heavy as 2-3 kg – much heavier than their own body weight.

▲ FISHY DIET

An African marsh harrier grabs a fish from a river near Natal, South Africa. Most marsh harriers live mainly on amphibians, small mammals, reptiles and insects.

Steller's sea eagle (*Haliaeetus pelagicus*)

▲ BEST FOOT FORWARD

A Steller's sea eagle extends both legs, talons at the ready, as it swoops down to take a fish. This is the largest of the fishing birds of prey, and it has an exceptionally fearsome bill. It lives around the coasts of the Pacific Ocean in Russia and China, where its favourite food is Pacific salmon. It will also take geese and hares.

Did you know? Bald eagles catch fish that are heavier than their own weight.

▲ HIGH LOOKOUT

An osprey, or fish hawk, surveys the water below from its untidy treetop nest. This clever fisher supports a number of other birds, such as fish eagles and terns, that rob it of its catch.

▲ AFRICAN ADVENTURES

An African fish eagle goes in for the kill over a lake in central Africa. The eagle pushes its feet forward during the dive and spreads both wings wide to slow the descent. The bird then plucks the unfortunate fish from the surface of the water and returns to feed on a nearby perch.

Focus on

The osprey is outstanding among the fishing birds of prey. Its acceleration is fast and spectacular, beginning high in the air and ending dramatically in the water. Sometimes it will submerge itself completely, unlike other fishing raptors. It feeds in lakes and rivers, and along estuaries and sea coasts. It takes freshwater fish, such as pike and trout. Marine sources of food include herring and flatfish. Although the osprey is a very skilful hunter, not all of its dives are successful. On average, it has to make three or four dives before it succeeds in making a kill. Ospreys may make up to four kills a day to feed themselves, but they need to catch more fish if they are very hungry or when they are feeding chicks in the nest.

1 The osprey soars over the lake, looking for fish swimming close to the water's surface. Once it spots its prey, the osprey falls like a stone out of the sky, gaining speed all the time. It opens out its wings to slow it down seconds before it hits the surface of the water. It brings its feet forwards as it enters the water's surface.

2 The osprey's outstretched feet pierce the surface of the water and thrust towards the fish with open claws. The fish can be nearly a metre down, and the osprey has to plunge right into the water to reach it. This time, however, the fish manages to avoid the hunter's clutches, and the bird looks as if it is taking a bath! In a shower of spray, the osprey struggles back into the air to try again.

Going Fishing

3 The next fish the osprey spies is swimming at the water's surface. Undeterred by the previous failure, the bird judges its dive well, and soon the fish is gripped in the osprey's sharp talons. The spiny surface of the osprey's feet provides extra gripping force and prevents the slippery prey from getting free, no matter how much it wriggles.

4 With powerful beats of its wings, the osprey pulls the fish out of the water. Its feet hold the fish's body head-first to cut down air resistance during the flight.

5 The osprey flies back to its perch. On the way, the bird might get attacked by pirates, birds that harry the osprey and force it to drop its catch, which they then pounce on.

6 With its catch in its claws, the osprey lands on its perch. There it uses its sharp bill to slice through the tough scales and skin of the fish to feast on the tasty flesh.

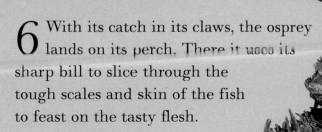

The Scavengers

Most birds of prey kill prey to eat, but many also scavenge on carrion (dead animals) when they find it. For example, the golden eagle feeds mainly on carrion during winter months, when its usual prey is scarce. However, one group of birds, called vultures, scavenges almost entirely on carrion. Vultures have sharp, sturdy bills for slicing through hides and tearing at meat and sinews. Some have heads, and often their necks, naked of feathers to prevent them becoming caked with blood. Their feet are broad for walking, but weak and with flat claws, because they do not need them to kill. Vultures are noted for their high, soaring flight on long, broad wings. They ride on thermals — warm air currents rising from the ground. They can spot carrion many kilometres away with their excellent eyesight.

▲ **AT THE SEASIDE**
This Andean condor soars in search of carrion over cliffs on the Pacific coast of South America. Its diet also includes a lot of fish. It has slightly longer wings than the Californian condor, with a wingspan of over 3 m.

▼ **BEARDED BONEBREAKER**
The lammergeier is also named the bearded vulture due to the black bristles on its face. It is famous for its habit of breaking bones by dropping them on rocks. It eats the bone fragments and the nutritious marrow inside.

Bearded vulture (*Gypaetus barbatus*)

▲ **CRACKING EGGS**
An Egyptian vulture uses a stone in its beak to crack the hard shell of an egg. It might be smaller than other vultures, but it seems more intelligent. It is the only tool-user among birds of prey. Ostrich eggs are among its favourite food.

◀ ON PATROL

European griffon vultures soar high in the sky using their long, broad wings. They keep a lookout for signs of carrion down below as they fly. Griffon vultures are common in the mountainous regions of southern Europe and northern Africa, often living in large flocks.

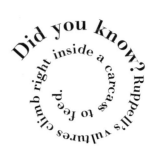

Did you know? Ruppell's vultures climb right inside a carcass to feed.

▶ SUNBATHING

A white-backed vulture stands with its wings wide open, sunning itself in the scorching heat of the African savanna. Many vultures do this, probably to allow their feathers to dry after bathing. They also do this to lose heat through the increased surface area of their spread wings.

▼ COLOURFUL KING

The king vulture has the most colourful and unusual head of all vultures. It is found in Central and South America, where it can be seen soaring over the rainforests and among the high peaks of the Andes mountains in search of carrion.

King vulture
(*Sarcoramphus papa*)

▲ TUCKING IN

A group of white-backed vultures tucks into the carcass of a freshly killed animal on the plains of Zimbabwe, southern Africa. These vultures soar and wheel high in the sky and are attracted to carrion when they see other vultures gathering around it. With their long, naked necks, they reach deeper inside carcasses to feed than some other vultures.

Going Courting

Males and females of most bird species usually get together once a year to mate and produce young. Then as soon as the young birds mature into adults, they too go off to find a mate. Some birds of prey stay with their mate for life. However, courting still takes place every year. This helps strengthen the bond between the two birds. In courtship displays there is usually much calling to each other, with the birds close together. The male may offer the female prey it has caught. Since most birds of prey are superb fliers, however, the most spectacular courtship displays take place in the air. The birds may perform acrobatic dances, or fly side by side, then swoop at each other and even clasp talons. The male may also drop prey whilst in flight for the female to dive and catch in an extravagant game of courtship feeding.

▲ **THE MARRIED COUPLE**
Like most birds of prey, American bald eagles usually mate for life. They occupy the same nest year after year, gradually adding to it each time they return to breed.

◀ **TOGETHERNESS**
Secretary birds become inseparable for life once they have paired up. Their courtship flights are most impressive, as they fly through the sky with their long tails streaming behind them. The birds also sleep side by side in their nest. They use their nests as living quarters throughout the year, not just during the breeding season.

▲ BEARING GIFTS

A male barn owl has caught a mouse and presents it to his mate back in the nest. This behaviour is called courtship feeding. It helps strengthen the bond between the pair. It is also preparation for the time when the male will have to feed the female when she is nest-bound and incubating their eggs.

▼ BALANCING ACT

A pair of ospreys struggle to keep their balance as they mate on a high perch. While the female turns her tail to one side, the male lowers his tail and presses his cloaca (sexual organ) against hers. His sperm can then be transferred to her body, and she can lay fertilized eggs that will hatch into chicks.

Did you know? Peregrines spend hours performing an amazing courtship flight.

▲ CARACARAS ON DISPLAY

A pair of striated caracaras call to one another by their nest. They are no longer courting but raising young. Mated pairs display like this frequently to strengthen the bond between them. Caracaras can raise two broods (groups of chicks hatched together) a year in South America, but in Florida, they are usually single-brooded.

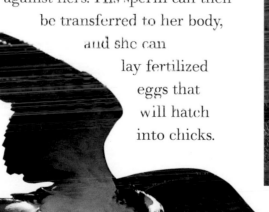

Osprey (*Pandion haliaetus*)

▲ FACE TO FACE

A pair of Egyptian vultures stand face to face on the ground in an elaborate courtship display. In addition to their ground-based display, the pair also perform spectacular aerial displays. They fly, climb and dive close together, often presenting each other their talons.

Building Nests and Laying Eggs

Courtship displays help the male and female birds to bond. They also help establish the pair's territory, the area in which they hunt. Within this territory, the birds build a nest in which the female lays her eggs. Birds of prey usually nest far apart, because they need a large hunting area. However, some species, including griffon vultures and lesser kestrels, nest in colonies. Birds of prey choose many different nesting sites, in caves and on cliffs, in barns and the disused nests of other birds, on the ground or high up in trees. The nests themselves may be simple scrapes on a ledge, no more than a bare place for the eggs to rest in. Other nests are elaborate structures built of branches and twigs. Many birds return to the same nest with the same mate every year, adding to it until it becomes a massive structure.

▲ CAMOUFLAGE COLOURS

This hen harrier is nesting on the ground among vegetation. The female, pictured brooding (sitting on her eggs), has the typical mottled-brown plumage of ground-nesting birds. This makes her hard to spot on the nest. The male often feeds the female in the air. He calls her to him, then drops the prey for her to catch.

Bonelli's eagle
(*Hieraaetus fasciatus*)

◄ SETTING UP HOME

A female Bonelli's eagle repairs her clifftop, keeping a careful watch over her young chick. If there are no cliffs in her territory, the female will build her nest at the top of a tall tree. The nests measure just under 2 m in diameter, and they are used year after year. You can see that scientists have ringed this chick's leg.

▶ GO AWAY!

With its wings spread wide to make it look bigger, a barn owl adopts a threatening pose to protect his nest. The female has already laid several eggs, which she will incubate for just over a month. During this time, the male feeds her, usually with rats, mice or voles, but sometimes with insects and small birds. If food is plentiful, the pair may raise two broods a year.

◀ IN A SCRAPE

On a cliff ledge, this peregrine falcon has made a simple nest called a scrape, clearing a small patch of ground to nest on. Many peregrines use traditional nesting sites, where birds have made their homes for centuries. Others have adapted to life in the city, making their scrapes on the ledges of skyscrapers, office buildings and churches.

◀ FULL UP

A secretary bird comes in to land on the huge tree-top nest of a colony of social weaver birds in search of its own nesting site. As this tree is full, the bird will have to choose another site in which to nest. It prefers low thorny trees such as the acacia. It makes its nest out of sticks, lining it with soft grass.

Secretary bird
(*Sagittarius serpentarius*)

▲ SECOND-HAND

A disused raven's nest has been adopted by this peregrine falcon. Peregrines do not build their own nest but often lay eggs in nests abandoned by other birds. The eggs are incubated by both parents. Falcon eggs are pale reddish-brown, unlike those of most other raptors, which are white or speckled.

Focus on

Once a pair of birds has mated the female lays her eggs. The number of eggs laid depends on the species. Large raptors, such as eagles, lay one or two eggs. Smaller raptors, such as kestrels, may lay up to 8 eggs. The eggs have to be incubated (kept warm) after they have been laid so that the baby birds can develop inside. This is done by one of the birds brooding (sitting on the eggs) in the nest all the time. Brooding is done usually by the female. The male's job is to bring the female food. Incubation times vary widely, from less than a month for small falcons to nearly two months for eagles and vultures.

1 A young Mauritius kestrel chick develops inside its egg, feeding on the nutrients surrounding it. Once the chick has grown enough, it begins to chip away at the shell with a projection on its bill called an egg tooth. In time, it makes a little hole, called a pip.

2 Pipping puts the chick in touch with the outside world, and its lungs breathe in the outside air. The chick rests for several hours and then starts hammering away with its egg tooth next to the first pip. After a while the chick twists around and starts hammering again. It does this until it has chipped right round the shell.

3 With the shell cracked, the chick starts its fight to break out. It presses its feet against the lower part of the shell and heaves with its shoulders against the upper part. Soon the top of the egg breaks off, and the head of the chick becomes visible.

Hatching Out

4 The chick kicks and heaves as it continues its fight to escape from the shell, resting frequently to regain its strength. Soon its head is free, then a wing and finally a leg. The chick prepares itself for a last push.

5 With all its remaining strength, the chick forces its body away from the shell. It lies almost motionless, wet and nearly naked, weak and helpless. The chick will need to rest for several hours before it has the strength to beg for food. This can be a dangerous time for the chick. It might be trampled by clumsy parents.

6 When the newly hatched chick dries out, its body is covered with sparse, fluffy down. This early down is not enough to keep the chick warm, so it has to snuggle up to its mother in the nest. Gradually, a thicker cover of down grows, which can be seen on these two-week-old kestrel chicks. A full covering of downy feathers will keep them warm and allow their mother to leave the nest.

A Chick's Life

When chicks hatch out, they find it difficult to move. They are unable to stand, and just sit on their ankles. Their bodies are covered with fine down, which cannot keep them warm. So they need their mother's warmth to stay alive. That is why she still does not move from the nest. The male continues to bring food, which she tears and feeds to the chicks. After a couple of weeks, a thicker down grows on the chicks' bodies to keep them warm, and the female can leave the nest and go hunting again. Soon the chicks grow strong enough to stand up and move about. In species where the eggs hatch at different times, older chicks beg the most food and grow strongest. This can result in the death of the weaker chicks.

▲ **CHICK AND RAT**
A barn owl chick is feeding on a rat its parents have caught. The chick is about six weeks old, and already the well-defined face patch characteristic of all owls has begun to appear.

◀ **SITTING PRETTY**
A secretary bird and its chick rest in their nest in a thorny tree on the African savanna. First, the parents feed the chick on regurgitated liquids. Later, they regurgitate rodents, insects and snakes into the nest for the chick to eat. The chick is fully feathered in five weeks and stays in the nest for about a month longer.

◀ FEEDING TIME

In its nest high up in a tall tree, a female booted eagle feeds its chick. The chick is several weeks old and still covered in thick down, but its feathers are beginning to appear. Both parents feed the chick, often hunting the same prey together. The booted eagle is one of the smallest eagles, with its body measuring about 50 cm from head to tail.

▼ LEMMING FEAST

A lemming is the next meal for this snowy owl chick. Lemmings are the staple (usual) diet of this owl. When lemmings are in plentiful supply, snowy owls may raise as many as eight chicks at a time. The eggs are laid over a considerable period of time, so there is a noticeable size difference between the young owls in large clutches.

Snowy owl
(*Nyctea scandiaca*)

▲ THREE IN A HOLE

Three kestrel chicks peer out of their nest in a hole in a tree. By the time they are a month old, they will have left the nest and be flying. It will take them up to another five weeks to copy their parents and master the art of hovering in the air to scan for prey.

Raising the Young

Young birds of prey remain in the nest for different periods, depending on the species. The young of smaller birds, such as merlins, are nest-bound for only about eight weeks. The young of larger species, such as the golden eagle, stay in the nest for more than three months. Young vultures may stay for over five months. As the chicks grow, their thick down moults to reveal their proper feathers. They become stronger and start to exercise their wings by standing up and flapping them. Shortly before they leave the nest, they make their first flight. This greatest step in the life of a young bird is called fledging. It takes weeks or even months before the fledglings (trainee fliers) have learned the flying and hunting skills they need to catch prey. During this time, they are still dependent on their parents for all their food.

▲ TAKING OFF
A young kestrel launches itself into the air. It is fully grown but still has its juvenile plumage. Other adults recognize the plumage, so they do not drive the young bird away.

▼ GROWING UP
The pictures below show three stages in the early life of a tawny owl. At four weeks, the chick is a fluffy ball of down. At seven weeks, it is quite well feathered. At 12 weeks, it is fully feathered and can fly.

4 weeks old

7 weeks old

12 weeks old

Pygmy falcon adult

Pygmy falcon juvenile
(*Poliohierax
semitorquatus*)

◄ BIG PYGMY

This pygmy falcon parent is still feeding its chick,
which is as big as the parent is. In the early
stages of the chick's life, the male pygmy
falcon supplies all the food, while the
female keeps the chick warm in the nest.
Then both adults feed the fledgling, until
the young bird learns to catch insects for itself.
This skill can take up to two months to master.

► MONTH-OLD KESTREL CHICKS

Two young kestrels huddle
together near their nest in
an old farm building. They
are fully feathered and
almost ready to take their
first flight. However, it could
be another month before
they learn to hunt.

Tawny owl
(*Strix aluco*)

◄ JUST PRACTISING

This tawny owl is still unable to fly.
It is flapping its wings up and down
to exercise and strengthen the
pectoral (chest) muscles that will
enable it to fly. As these muscles get
stronger, the young bird will
sometimes lift off its perch.
Eventually, often on a windy day, the
owl will find itself flying in the
air. On this first flight, it will not travel
far. Within days, it will be
flying just like
its parents.

43

Open Country

Birds of prey are found almost everywhere in the world. However, each species prefers a different kind of habitat, in which it can hunt certain kinds of prey. This prevents too much competition for the food resources available. Many species prefer open country habitats. Imperial and golden eagles hunt in open mountainous country. On the bleak expanses of the Arctic tundra the gyrfalcon and snowy owl are the most successful predators. The vast savanna lands of eastern and southern Africa are the home of many vultures. Here, there are rich pickings on the carcasses of grazing animals killed by big cats such as the cheetah and lion. Areas where farming is practised are common hunting grounds for kestrels and harriers.

▲ **GROUND NESTER**
A young Montagu's harrier spreads its wings in the nest. Like other harriers, it nests among thick vegetation. This harrier lives on open moors and farmland throughout Europe, northern Africa and Asia.

Did you know? The gyrfalcon is the largest falcon, up to 62 cm from head to tail.

◄ **TUNDRA HUNTER**
A gyrfalcon devours its prey. This bird lives in the cold, wide-open spaces of the Arctic tundra, in Alaska, northern Canada and northern Europe. The bird in the picture is a young bird with dark, juvenile plumage. The adult is much paler – grey above and white underneath. Some birds are almost pure white and blend in perfectly with their snowy habitat.

▲ VULTURES AT THE CAPE

The Cape vultures of southern Africa inhabit the clifftops and hilly regions around the Cape of Good Hope. They have broad wings that enable them to soar effortlessly on the warm air currents rising from the hot land below. Often, several birds soar together, watching out for a meal to share and guarding their territory against other vultures.

▼ KILLING FIELDS

A common buzzard feeds on carrion—a dead rabbit that it has recently found. Buzzards, or buteos, are found in open and lightly wooded country throughout the world. They live in both lowland and highland areas and feed mainly on small mammals.

◀ PLAINS WALKER

The secretary bird can be found in most savanna, or grassland, habitats in Africa south of the Sahara desert. Its long legs enable it to walk through all but the tallest grass. It avoids forests, but it does build its nest in trees.

▼ SUNNING ON THE SAVANNA

A juvenile bateleur eagle suns itself on a tree in the sparse savanna (open plains) of Africa, keeping a watchful eye for small mammals and reptiles. It takes six years for a juvenile to reach full maturity.

Bateleur eagle
(*Terathopius ecaudatus*)

45

Woodlands and Wetlands

Honey buzzard (*Pernis apivorus*)

The world's woodlands make good hunting grounds for many different birds of prey. The sparrowhawk and goshawk, and the common and honey buzzards, all make their homes in woodland habitats. Many owls prefer a wooded habitat, nesting in both coniferous and broadleafed trees. The most formidable forest predators, however, are the enormous South American harpy eagle and the Philippine eagle. They live in rainforests and hunt monkey prey high in the treetops. Freshwater and marine wetlands are the territory of the sea and fishing eagles and the osprey. Among the smaller birds of prey, peregrines hunt around sea cliffs, while marsh harriers hunt among the reed beds of freshwater marshes. In Africa and Asia, the fishing owls make their homes in woodlands close to the coast or by inland waterways.

▲ FOREST FEEDER

The honey buzzard is commonly found in the deciduous forests of Europe, where it feeds mainly on the larvae of bees and wasps. It is quite a small bird, with a delicate bill suited to its diet.

◀ IN THE MARSHES

Three marsh harrier chicks peep out of their reed nest in a swampy region of Poland. Marsh harriers are the largest harriers, measuring up to 55 cm from head to tail. They hunt in the reed beds and on open farmland nearby. These fearsome hunters will eat most birds, small mammals, reptiles, and amphibians.

◄ DOWN IN THE JUNGLE

The harpy eagle lives in the thick forests and jungles of Central and South America. It is an awesome predator, picking animals as big as sloths and monkeys from the trees, as well as birds such as parrots. Harpy eagles grow up to a metre from head to tail. They have huge talons to grip their heavy prey.

▲ DAYLIGHT OWL

A hawk owl perches on a tree stump. The hawk owl lives in the massive conifer forests of northern Canada and Alaska. It can often be seen in daylight.

▼ EAGLE AT SEA

This white-bellied sea eagle lives high on the clifftops of an island in Indonesia, South-east Asia. Like other sea eagles, it takes fish from both coastal and inland waters and also feeds on carrion. This bird will also eat poisonous sea snakes.

▲ FLEET FLIER

The sparrowhawk is found in the woodlands of Europe and Asia. It flies swiftly and close to the ground, using the dense vegetation as cover. However, it sometimes hunts like a peregrine, circling high and then diving steeply at its prey.

On the Move

Every bird of prey maintains a territory in which it can feed and breed. There is usually no room for the parents' offspring, so they have to forge a new territory themselves. The parents may stay in their breeding area all year long if there is enough food. If not, they may migrate (move away) to somewhere warmer in winter, sometimes because their prey have themselves migrated. For example, peregrines that bred on the tundra in northern Europe fly some 14,000 kilometres to spend winter in South Africa.

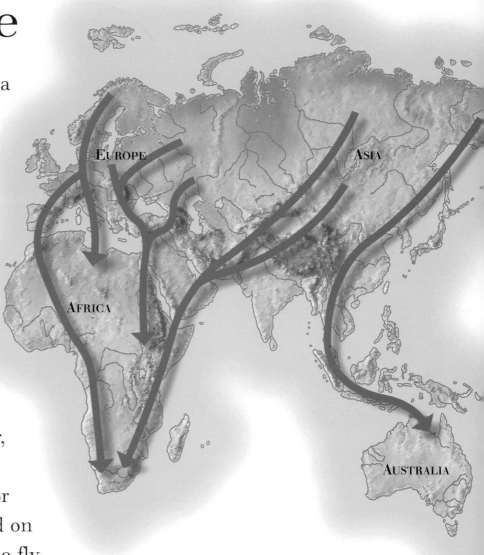

◄ **ESCAPING SOUTH**
The rough-legged buzzard is slightly larger than its cousin, the common buzzard. It breeds in far northern regions of the world in the spring, both on the treeless tundra and the forested taiga. In the autumn, it migrates south to escape the cold Arctic winter.

▲ **FLIGHT PATHS**
Birds avoid migrating over large stretches of water. There are fewer uplifting air currents over water than there are over land. So many migration routes pass through regions where there is a convenient land bridge or a short sea crossing. Panama, in Central America, is one such area. Gibraltar, in southern Europe, is another.

▼ JUST PASSING

This sooty falcon was spotted on its way south to the island of Madagascar, where it spends the winter. In spring, it will return to northeast Africa or Israel to breed.

Sooty falcon (*Falco concolor*)

KEY

→ migration routes of birds of prey

NORTH AMERICA

SOUTH AMERICA

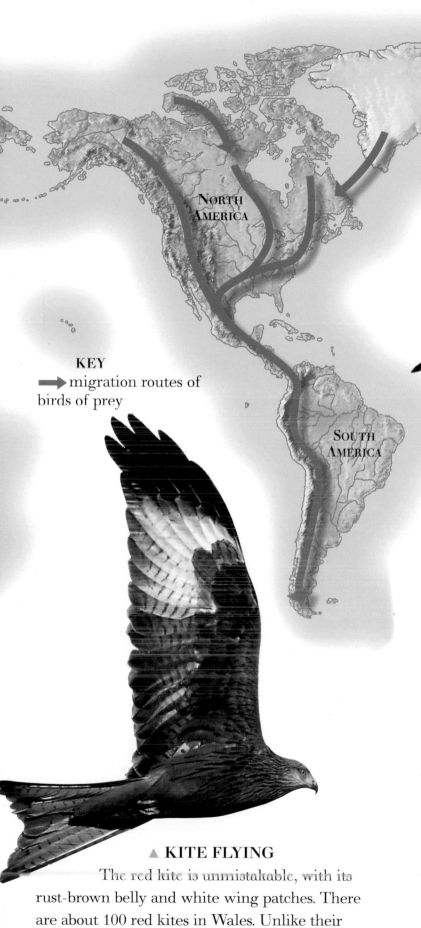

▲ KITE FLYING

The red kite is unmistakable, with its rust-brown belly and white wing patches. There are about 100 red kites in Wales. Unlike their continental European cousins, those that breed in Wales do not usually migrate south in winter.

▲ GRACEFUL FLOCK

Graceful kites fly over an Indian village during their annual migration from Asia to warmer winter quarters in southern Africa. They will cover hundreds of kilometres a day.

Orders and Families

There are more than 400 species of birds of prey. Each is different in size, colouring, behaviour and feeding pattern from every other species. Birds of prey fall into two major groupings, or orders. The diurnal raptors, the day-time hunters, belong to the order Falconiformes. The owls, the night-hunters, belong to the order Strigiformes. Within each order, similar kinds of birds are classed together in family groups. In the Falconiformes, there are five families. The secretary bird and the osprey have a family each. New World vultures form another family, and the falcons and caracaras another. But by far the largest family, containing more than 200 species, is the so-called accipiters, which include eagles, Old World vultures, kites, hawks and buzzards.

▲ NIGHT-HUNTERS

This great grey owl is one of about 130 species of owls. Most, but not all, are nocturnal (night) hunters. Owls belong to the order Strigiformes and are not related to the other birds of prey.

Roman Eagle

To the ancient Romans, the eagle symbolized power, nobility, strength and courage. When the Roman army marched into battle, one soldier at the head of each legion (group of soldiers) carried a golden eagle on a standard (see left). The Roman name for the eagle was aquila. Today, this name is given to a family of eagles, including the magnificent golden eagle.

► THE CARACARAS

This striated caracara lives in the Falkland Islands. It is the member of a group within the falcon family. Caracaras are large, long-legged birds found from the southern United States to southern South America. Unlike true falcons, they often hunt on the ground.

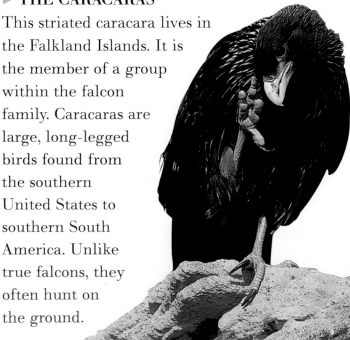

▼ ALL ALONE

There is only one species of osprey the world over. This one is nesting in Maryland, in the eastern USA, where it is known as a fish hawk. Some of the largest colonies of ospreys are found in north-eastern Africa.

▲ TALL SECRETARY

The secretary bird looks like no other bird of prey, so it is not surprising that it has a family all to itself. Its distinctive features are a crest on its head, very long tail and legs, and short, stubby toes.

▼ OLD WORLD VULTURES

These white-backed vultures live in southern Africa. They belong to a family of some 14 species of vultures, found in the "Old World", that is, Europe, Asia and Africa. Like all vultures, they live largely on carrion, often the remains of prey killed by big cats like lions.

King vulture
(*Sarcoramphus papa*)

White-backed vulture
(*Gyps africanus*)

▲ VULTURES OF THE NEW WORLD

The king vulture displays its impressive 1·7-metre wingspan. This bird is the most colourful and maybe the most handsome vulture of all. It is one of the seven species of "New World" vultures, found in the Americas. The Andean and Californian condors are two other members of this group.

Focus on

Most eagles are very large, aggressive birds, preying on both small and large mammals, other birds and reptiles. Although some are hardly bigger than buzzards, they are in general fiercer and more active. Each eagle has a different lifestyle and hunting strategy. The golden eagle swoops down from on high mostly on mammal prey. The bald eagle takes mainly fish. The tawny eagle will eat anything. The most distinctive feature of the bateleur eagle is its acrobatic manoeuvres in the air. Its name comes from a French word meaning acrobat.

FAMILY LIFE

A bald eagle returns to its nest with a rock ptarmigan in its talons. Now it will tear strips of meat from its prey and feed them to its two offspring. These two eaglets are only a few weeks old and have just grown their thick second coat of down. They are still not strong enough to stand on their legs.

Bateleur eagle (juvenile)
(*Terathopius ecaudata*)

YOUNG AND OLD

For the first few years of its life, the bateleur eagle has drab brown juvenile plumage (*left*). But by the sixth year, it has acquired glorious adult plumage (*right*), which signals that it is now mature and ready to breed.

Bateleur eagle (adult)

Eagles

MARTIAL LORE

A martial eagle swoops down from the skies to deliver a deadly blow to a monitor lizard basking in the searing-hot African savanna. This heavy bird, with its huge wingspan of up to 2.5 m, will often capture small animals, mostly reptiles, but it usually feeds on game birds. The martial eagle is persecuted by humans because it occasionally attacks domestic livestock such as chickens and goats.

TAWNY SCAVENGER

The tawny eagle of Africa is mainly a scavenger. It often joins a flock of vultures to feed on the carcasses of prey killed by big cats, such as the zebra in this photograph. It also frequently steals prey from other raptors.

Golden eagle
(*Aquila chrysaetos*)

MASTER OF THE MOUNTAINS

A golden eagle opens its wings wide. They span nearly 2.5 m. This magnificent bird gets its name from the golden tinges on its head and neck feathers. It lives in remote mountains around the world and feeds on birds, mammals and carrion.

Fellow Hunters

Kookaburra
(*Dacelo gigas*)

▲ **KOOKABURRA CATCH**

A snake makes a good meal for this Australian kookaburra. It eats more or less anything, from frogs to small mammals and other small birds.

Birds of prey are probably the most feared hunters of the bird world. However, they are not the only birds that hunt live prey. Other birds catch insects and worms, amphibians and fish, and even small mammals and other birds. Most common are the insect-eaters, such as the bee-eater and the flycatcher. Wading birds, such as the oystercatcher, feed on worms and crustaceans, while herons eat amphibians and fish. Skimmers, pelicans and all kinds of seabirds live mainly on fish. Many seabirds prey on the chicks of other species, as do magpies on land. Many birds, especially those belonging to the crow family, will eat small mammals and carrion. However, none of these birds is classed as a bird of prey, for they lack the formidable sharp, hooked bill and lethal, taloned feet of the raptor.

▲ **BIG BILL**

The turkey-sized African ground hornbill loves to eat snakes, even very poisonous ones such as cobras. It kills them by repeatedly squeezing up and down their bodies with the tip of its large, powerful bill.

▼ **HUNTER-SCAVENGER**

A harvest mouse has just been killed by this common crow. The crow will also eat insects and the eggs and young of other birds, as well as carrion. Other members of the crow family, such as jackdaws and magpies, have a similar diet.

Crow
(*Corvus corone*)

▶ STANDING IN WAIT

The great blue heron of North America stands absolutely still at the water's edge, scanning the water for fish as they swim by. When it sees a fish, the heron thrusts its long bill into the water lightning-fast and grabs it with deadly accuracy. It hits the fish on the ground to kill it, before swallowing it head-first. Herons also eat frogs and mammals such as voles.

◀ BROWN BULLY

A brown skua swoops down to take a giant petrel chick on the remote Atlantic island of South Georgia. Skuas are always on the lookout for eggs and chicks left in nests whilst the parent birds are away feeding. They are also known for harrying (chasing) birds that have just been fishing. They make them disgorge (throw up) their food and eat it themselves.

Did you know? Butcher birds impale their prey on sharp thorns.

▼ DEADLY DIVER

Perching on a branch, a kingfisher prepares to eat a recent catch. This bird feeds almost entirely on fish. It perches near the water's edge and dives in head-first when it spots its prey. The kingfisher then beats the fish on a branch until it stops wriggling. Only then is it swallowed.

Kingfisher
(*Alcedo atthis*)

Falconry

Hunting with birds of prey is called falconry or hawking. It has been a popular sport in the Middle East for thousands of years. Today it has many followers in other parts of the world. Falconers use a variety of birds for hunting. Some prefer to use true falcons, or longwings, such as peregrines. However, shortwings, such as goshawks, and the broadwings, such as buzzards, are also used. Falconers need skill and patience to train a bird. First they must gain the bird's trust so that it will sit and feed on the fist. This process is known as manning. Then the bird must be trained to get fit and to learn to chase prey. Falconers fly birds on long lines, called creances, before allowing them to fly free. Other special equipment used in falconry includes jesses (leg fastenings), hoods (blindfolds) and lures (imitation prey).

Hood

Perch

▲ IN THE DARK

This picture displays two essential features of falconry equipment, or furniture. The leather hood is used when the bird is on the perch and also when it is taken out hunting. Falcons such as the one above need a flat block perch to rest on.

▶ ARAB SPORT

An Arab falconer proudly displays a falcon as it perches on a strong leather glove on his fist. Falconry has been a popular sport in the Middle East ever since it began there more than 3,000 years ago. The favourite birds of Arab falconers are the saker and the peregrine falcon.

▶ KITTED OUT

A lanner falcon is about to fly back to its handler. A leash is threaded through a ring (swivel) on the jess, which is attached to the leg of the falcon. A bell helps the falconer to locate the bird if it wanders.

Bell

Jess

▲ LURING AND STOOPING

Moving at speed, a lanner falcon chases a lure being swung by a falconer. Falconers use lures to get falcons fit and agile and teach them to be persistent hunters. They swing the lure around their bodies or high in the air, tempting the bird to fly at it and stoop (dive swiftly).

Did you know? A hawk's bent flight feathers can be straightened by steaming.

▲ ON THE FIST

The first stage in training a bird is to get it to sit on the fist whilst tethered. When it first does so, the bird should be rewarded with a piece of meat. Soon, the bird should actively step up, then jump on the fist to feed.

▲ HAROLD GOES HAWKING

In a scene on the famous Bayeux tapestry, King Harold of England is seen riding with a hawk on his fist. The tapestry portrays events leading up to the Battle of Hastings and the conquest of England by the Normans in 1066. Hawking, or falconry, was a favourite sport of noblemen in the Middle Ages.

Under Threat

In the wild, birds of prey have few natural enemies except, perhaps, other birds of prey. In many habitats they are the top predator. They have only one thing to fear – humans. Over the centuries, people have hunted raptors as vermin (pests) because they have occasionally killed domestic livestock, such as birds raised for game. Recently humans have been killing birds of prey indirectly by using pesticides on seeds and crops. When birds catch contaminated animals, pesticides build up in their own bodies and eventually poison them, causing death. Many birds of prey are now protected by law. This, and the safer use of farm chemicals, has led to a recovery in the numbers of several species. However, the indiscriminate shooting of migrating birds is still a threat, as is the destruction of forest habitats in which they live.

▲ **TRIGGER HAPPY**
A shooting enthusiast takes aim. A dog stands nearby, ready to retrieve the fallen bird. Raptors are shot by irresponsible hunters every year, especially as they flock together when migrating.

▲ **GRIM WARNING**
A dead hawk is left dangling on a piece of rope. This age-old practice is used by gamekeepers and farmers to warn off other birds of prey or vermin (pests) such as crows.

◀ **PHILIPPINE EAGLE**
The Philippine eagle is one of the rarest of all birds of prey. This is because the dense tropical forest in which it lives is rapidly being destroyed for farming and for humans to live. The eagle gets its name from the Philippine Islands, in Southeast Asia, where it lives. It eats mammals called lemurs, various kinds of birds and sometimes monkeys.

◀ **DEADLY CHEMICALS**
A sparrowhawk has been poisoned to death. It has preyed on smaller birds that have eaten seeds or insects sprayed with chemical pesticides. Gradually, the chemicals built up in the sparrowhawk's body until they made it ill, finally causing its death.

Did you know? Barn owls and kites are killed by eating poison-resistant rats.

Alice and the Griffin
A griffin sits next to Alice in a scene from Alice's Adventures in Wonderland. *The griffin is a mythical bird. According to Greek legend, it had the head and wings of an eagle but the body of a lion.*

▲ **HIT AND RUN**
A barn owl lies dead at the roadside, battered by a passing vehicle the night before. Motor vehicles kill thousands of birds every day and every night. At night, owls often hunt for small prey, such as mice and voles, in roadside verges and hedges. Their habit of slow-flying close to the ground puts them in danger from passing cars and trucks.

Conservation

Conservationists aim to protect species of animals and birds that are in danger of extinction. They study the habitats, lifestyles and movements of birds of prey by catching them, putting rings around their legs and tracking their movements. They have also preserved many species that were on the brink of extinction by breeding them in captivity, then releasing the offspring back into the wild. Today there are study centres and sanctuaries worldwide, where birds of prey can be closely observed. Here the public also has the chance to see them in action. The future of many species of birds of prey is more secure in parts of the world where there is a "greener" approach to wildlife and the environment.

▲ UP THE POLE

Some birds prefer human-made structures to trees when it comes to nesting. In Glacier National Park, fake telephone posts were built for ospreys to nest on when experts found that nests on real posts caused line interference.

◀ THE RAREST

The Californian condor is the rarest of all birds of prey. It became extinct in the wild in the 1980s. The last few birds were taken into captivity, where they fortunately began to breed. Several pairs of Californian condors have already been released successfully back into the wild.

Californian condor
(Gymnogyps californianus)

▲ FLYING LESSONS

In 1998, firefighters abseiled down a 91 m cliff to rescue a three-month-old falcon. The fledgling's leg had become entangled in barbed wire. After being treated by a local vet, the falcon was taught to hunt and fly at a bird of prey centre in Newent, England, before being released back into the wild.

◀ ON THE LOOKOUT

Bird-watchers gather in the Everglades National Park in Florida, USA. This outstanding wetland habitat is now a conservation area. Visitors can spot many birds of prey, including America's national bird, the bald eagle.

▶ THE EAGLE'S RINGS

Bird-watchers put a ring on the leg of a Bonelli's eagle. The team have already measured, sexed and weighed the bird, and recorded where it was captured. The bird is released when all the recordings are taken. If it is caught again another year, the bird's condition and location can be compared to these records, helping to keep a check on the health and movements of the eagle population.

Did you know? Peregrines are no longer endangered in North America.

◀ HANDLE WITH CARE

Here in a Kenyan wildlife park, a bird handler is showing off a Crowned Eagle. Sanctuaries for birds of prey have been set up in many countries across the world. Visitors are often treated to spectacular flying displays by diverse raptors.

GLOSSARY

broadwing
A term used in falconry for birds with broad wings, such as buzzards.

carrion
The flesh of dead animals.

creance
A long line falconers use to train a bird before they let it fly free.

cloaca
The sexual organ of a bird.

diurnal
Active by day.

down
Fine, hairy feathers for warmth not flight. Young chicks have only down and no flight feathers.

egg tooth
A chalky projection a chick has on its bill when it is ready to hatch. It uses the tooth to cut the shell.

facial disc
A circle of tiny feathers around the face of an owl.

falconry
Flying falcons or hawks as a sport. Also called hawking.

fingers
Feathers at the ends of a bird's wings, which look rather like a human's fingers.

fledging
The time when a bird starts to fly. A fledgling is a bird that is just beginning to fly.

genus
A grouping of living things, smaller than a family, but larger than a species. The genus is the first word of the Latin name, e.g. in the King vulture's latin name *Sarcoramphus papa*, the genus is *Sarcoramphus*.

habitat
The kind of surroundings in which an animal usually lives.

harry
To intimidate another bird.

hybrid
In falconry, a hawk that is cross-bred – that is, its parents are of two different species, such as a saker and a peregrine falcon.

incubate
To sit on eggs to keep them warm so that baby birds will develop inside.

jess
A leather strip fastened round a hawk's leg by which it is held.

juvenile
A young bird, before it grows its adult plumage.

lift
The upward force acting on a bird's wings when it moves through the air. It supports the bird's weight.

longwing
A bird of the falcon family that has long, pointed wings.

lure
An imitation bird swung on a line to act as a target when training a falcon.

manning
Making a hawk tame by getting it used to people.

mantling
Standing over a kill with wings spread to hide it.

migration
Movement from place to place. Many birds of prey fly to warmer climates for the winter.

mobbing
When prey birds gang up against their predators and try to drive them away.

name
The same species (kind) of bird of prey often has a different common name in different countries. The bird called an osprey in Europe is often referred to as a fish hawk in North America. That is why birds are better identified by their scientific (Latin) name, which never alters.

nestling
A young bird before it has left the nest.

nocturnal
Active by night. Owls are
nocturnal birds of prey.

order
A major grouping of animals,
larger than a family. Owls belong
to the order Strigiformes; all
other birds of prey to the
order Falconiformes.

ornithologist
A person who studies birds.

pectorals
The powerful breast muscles of a
bird, used in flight.

pellet
A ball of indigestible matter
coughed up by birds of prey.

pip
The first tiny hole a hatching
chick makes in the eggshell.

piracy
When one bird harries another
to make it let go of prey it
has caught.

plumage
The covering of feathers on a
bird's body.

predator
An animal that hunts and kills
other animals for food.

prey
An animal that is hunted
for food.

raptor
Any bird of prey. From the Latin
rapere meaning to seize, grasp or
take by force.

regurgitate
Bring up food that has already
been swallowed.

ringing
Attaching a small ring to the leg
of a bird.

savanna
Regions of open grassland found
in places such as Africa.

scavenger
An animal that lives mainly on
the meat of dead animals.

scrape
A patch of ground cleared by a
bird to lay its eggs on.

sexual dimorphism
The difference in size between
male and female birds,
commonly found among falcons.

shortwing
In falconry, a true hawk, with
short wings.

soaring
Gliding high in the air on
outstretched wings, riding on
air currents.

species
Kind. Scientifically, a
species is the narrowest
grouping of living things,
smaller than a genus.

stooping
When a falcon dives on its
prey from on high at great
speed, with wings
nearly closed.

supraorbital ridge
A prominent ridge above the
eyes in birds of prey, rather like
an eyebrow.

taiga
Forested parts of far northern
regions of the world. Taiga lies
just south of the tundra.

thermal
A rising current of warm air, on
which vultures and other birds of
prey soar.

tropical
In the tropics, the region of the
world close to the Equator, where
the climate is hot and humid.

tundra
The cold, treeless land in far
northern regions of the world,
which is covered with snow for
much of the year.

wingspan
The distance across the wings,
from one wing-tip to the other.

INDEX

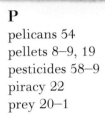